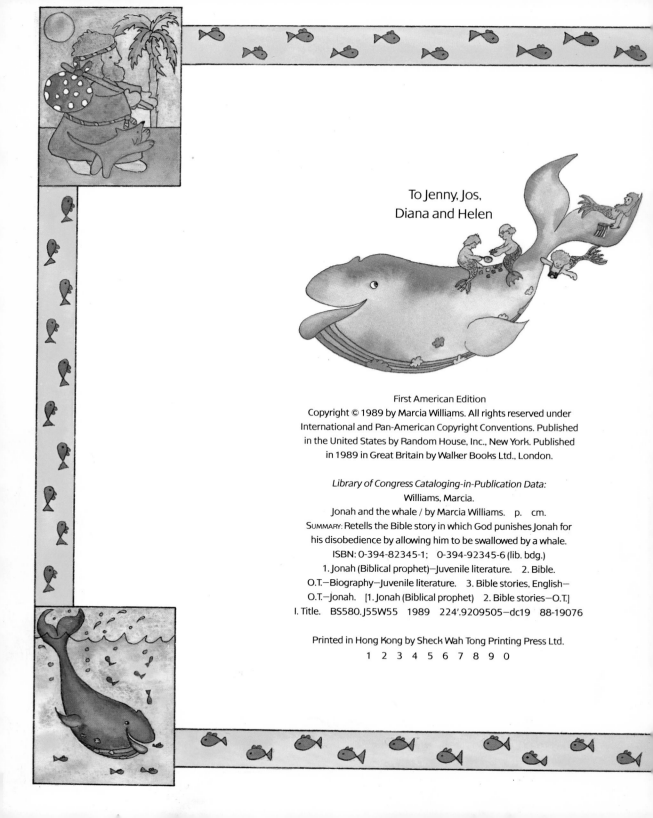

To Jenny, Jos,
Diana and Helen

First American Edition
Copyright © 1989 by Marcia Williams. All rights reserved under
International and Pan-American Copyright Conventions. Published
in the United States by Random House, Inc., New York. Published
in 1989 in Great Britain by Walker Books Ltd., London.

Library of Congress Cataloging-in-Publication Data:
Williams, Marcia.
Jonah and the whale / by Marcia Williams.   p.   cm.
SUMMARY: Retells the Bible story in which God punishes Jonah for
his disobedience by allowing him to be swallowed by a whale.
ISBN: 0-394-82345-1;   0-394-92345-6 (lib. bdg.)
1. Jonah (Biblical prophet)—Juvenile literature.   2. Bible.
O.T.—Biography—Juvenile literature.   3. Bible stories, English—
O.T.—Jonah.   [1. Jonah (Biblical prophet)   2. Bible stories—O.T.]
I. Title.   BS580.J55W55   1989   224'.9209505—dc19   88-19076

Printed in Hong Kong by Sheck Wah Tong Printing Press Ltd.
1   2   3   4   5   6   7   8   9   0

JONAH
AND THE
WHALE

WRITTEN AND ILLUSTRATED BY
MARCIA WILLIAMS

Random House 🏠 New York

Many, many moons ago

in a land of deserts and date palms

God spoke to a man named Jonah.

But Jonah did not believe God would do this.

He decided not to go. Instead he ran away.

He found a ship traveling to Tarshish,

in the opposite direction from Nineveh.

He paid his fare and went on board.

God was so angry with Jonah

that He sent a terrible storm.

The howling wind tore at the ship's sail.

The waves grew higher and higher,

tossing the ship up and down, up and down.

The sailors feared that the ship would break in two.

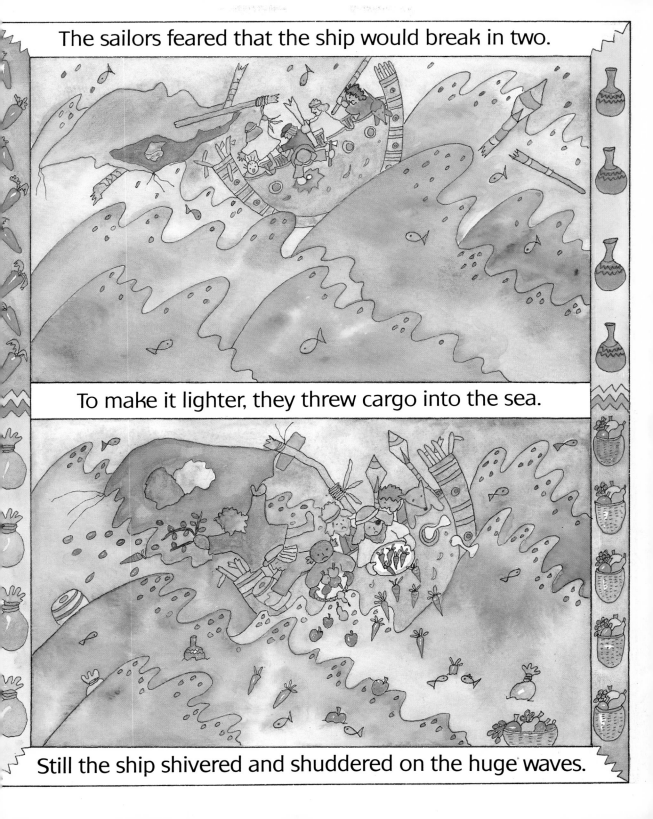

To make it lighter, they threw cargo into the sea.

Still the ship shivered and shuddered on the huge waves.

On the deck the sailors prayed to their gods.

Jonah was sleeping below

until the captain woke him.

"Jonah," he said, "pray to your God to save us!"

Jonah prayed, but the storm grew even fiercer.

The sailors and their captain were terrified.

Then Jonah told them that God had sent the storm

because he had not gone to Nineveh.

"If I give myself to the sea," said Jonah,

"I'm sure the waters will be calm again."

The sailors did not want Jonah to drown,

and they tried hard to row to land.

But in vain, for the sea became even wilder.

So, sadly, they threw Jonah overboard.

Instantly the raging waters grew calm.

Fearing for Jonah's life,

the sailors prayed to God for forgiveness.

Then they set sail again for Tarshish

on the still, clear waters.

But Jonah did not drown.

At first he floated.

Then he got caught in some weeds.

Jonah was dragged

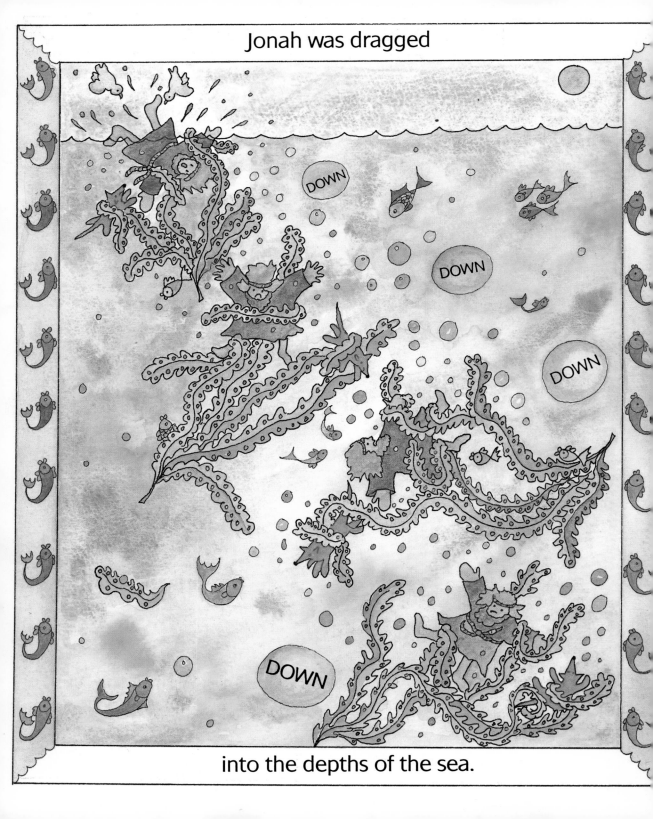

into the depths of the sea.

Just as he felt he was about to die,

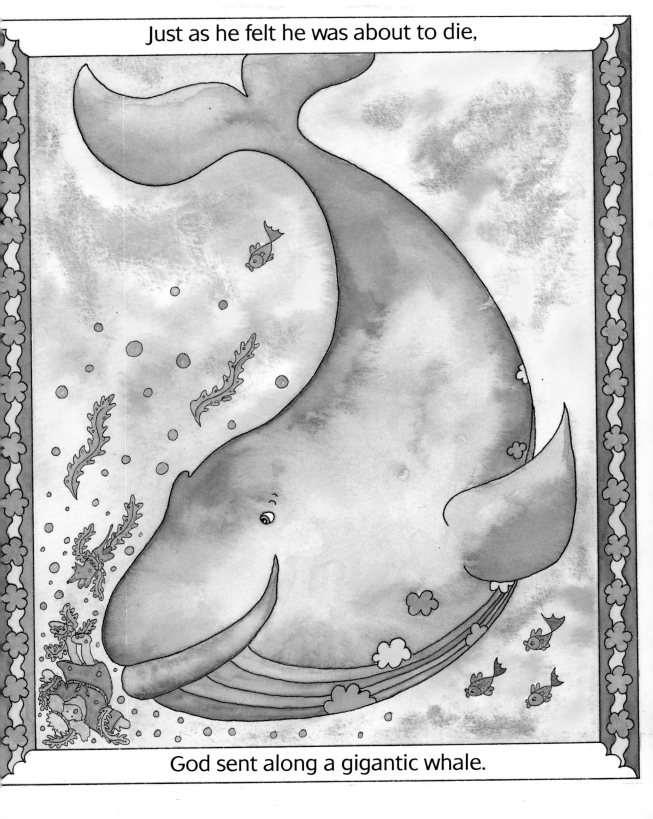

God sent along a gigantic whale.

The whale swallowed Jonah whole.

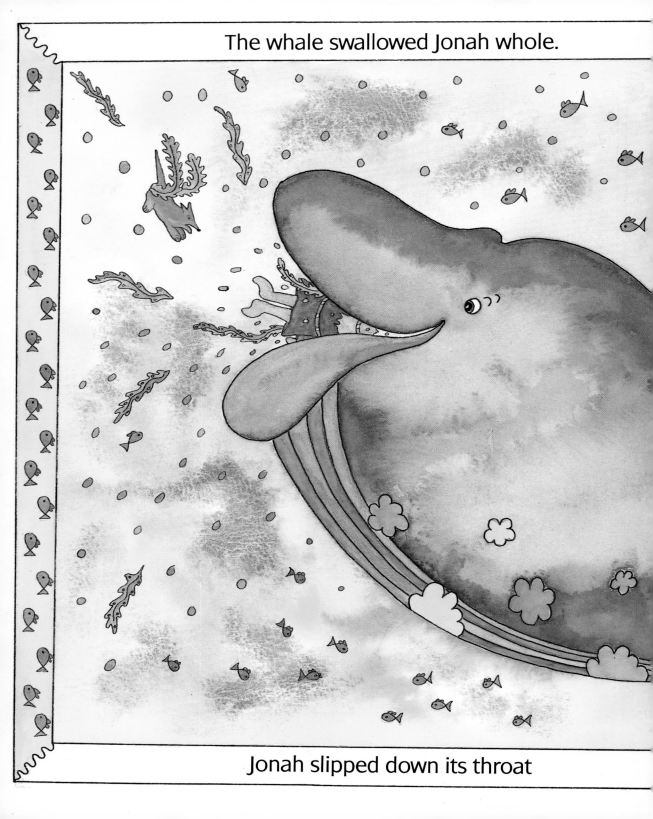

Jonah slipped down its throat

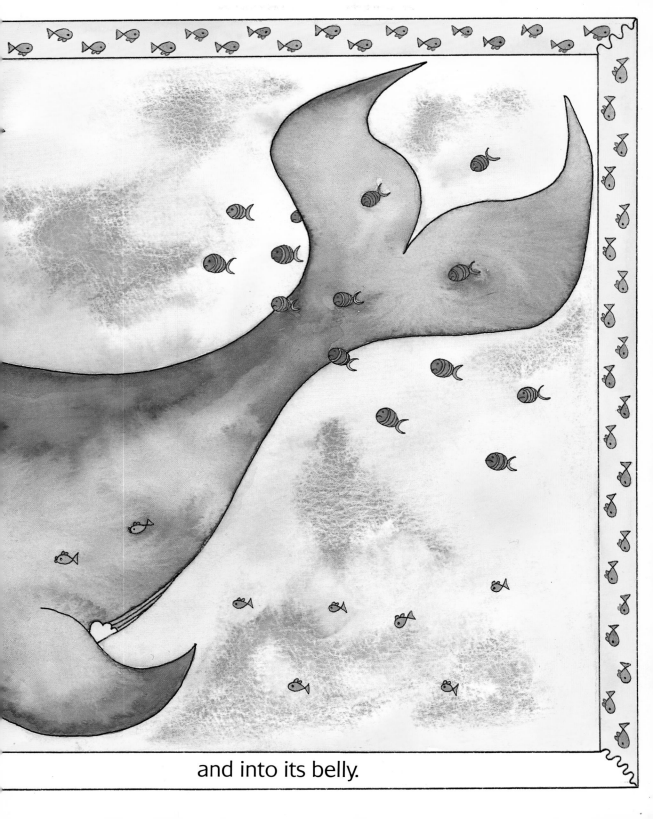

and into its belly.

It was cold and dark, and Jonah was afraid.

Three days and three nights passed.

Sometimes Jonah slept,

but mostly he prayed to God to forgive him.

At last God took pity on Jonah

and told the whale to spit him out.

Jonah landed on the earth with a bump.

He was very shaken

and could hardly stand on his feet,

but he was glad to be on dry land.

Then God spoke to Jonah again.

"Go to Nineveh," He said, "and warn the people

that in forty days their city will be destroyed

unless they become good and kind."

This time Jonah obeyed God.

He traveled to Nineveh and cried out God's warning.

The King and people of Nineveh believed Jonah.

They put on sackcloth and promised to repent.

When God saw this, he was happy to spare them.

Jonah and everyone who lived in Nineveh rejoiced.